Successful Telemarketing
in a week

Successful Telephone Selling

in a week

PATRICK FORSYTH

Hodder & Stoughton

A MEMBER OF THE HODDER HEADLINE GROUP

Orders: please contact Bookpoint Ltd, 39 Milton Park, Abingdon, Oxon OX14 4TD.
Telephone: (44) 01235 400414, Fax: (44) 01235 400454. Lines are open from 9.00 -
6.00, Monday to Saturday, with a 24 hour message answering service.
Email address: orders@bookpoint.co.uk

British Library Cataloguing in Publication Data
A catalogue record for this title is available from The British Library

ISBN 0 340 73026 9

First published 1998
Impression number   10 9 8 7 6 5 4 3 2 1
Year   2004 2003 2002 2001 2000 1999 1998

Typeset by Multiplex Techniques Ltd, St Mary Cray, Kent.
Printed in Great Britain for Hodder & Stoughton Educational, a division of
Hodder Headline Plc, 338 Euston Road, London NW1 3BH by Cox & Wyman Ltd,
Reading, Berkshire.

the Institute
of Management

F O U N D A T I O N

The Institute of Management (IM) exists to promote the development, exercise and recognition of professional management. The Institute embraces all levels of management from student to chief executive and supports its own Foundation which provides a unique portfolio of services for all managers, enabling them to develop skills and achieve management excellence.

For information on the various levels and benefits of membership, please contact:

Department HS
Institute of Management
Cottingham Road
Corby
Northants NN17 1TT
Tel: 01536 204222
Fax: 01536 201651

This series is commissioned by the Institute of Management Foundation.

CONTENTS

I N T R O D U C T I O N

Selling is an activity, a part of the marketing mix, which plays a vital part in bringing in, securing, holding and developing business. Much selling is face to face, and where this is the case, it is the field sales staff that make the final link with prospects and customers.

But other means of communication can also be used in selling. One of the main methods is communication by telephone. This can appear deceptively simple, just a matter of dialling and chatting personably about the product or service. Not so. Telephone contact, particularly persuasive telephone contact, can do as much harm as good. It demands the right approach, and considerable care, if it is to work well.

Viewed the right way, however, it can provide positive and powerful contact, either resulting in orders being taken during the call, or acting to set up and follow through the sales process and influence the future outcome.

This book looks at the various processes involved in selling on the telephone, dividing the coverage to provide seven manageable topics, one for each day of the week:

Sunday	The rationale
Monday	Creating the opportunity
Tuesday	The fundamentals
Wednesday	Handling incoming calls
Thursday	Taking the initiative
Friday	Developing repeat business
Saturday	Working with the field sales team

The rationale

Day One, and the first task is to get to grips with some
underlying factors about selling on the telephone. There are
both negative and positive elements to consider here. We
will get the negative ones out of the way first.

A bad image

Selling does not have a universally rosy image. Say you are
in selling, and for many people the image that comes to
mind is of enthusiastic chat or, at worst, arm twisting and
pushing inappropriate products at the wrong people.
Telephone selling can face a similar, or worse, problem.

Yet the image on page ten is actually only true of *bad* selling. If sales approaches, whether in person or on the telephone, are not appropriate, then they may well upset people. Specific factors can lead irrevocably to a negative response.

Bad selling is:

- not prepared or organised
- not focused on customer needs
- not directed to the individual
- not clear or well structured
- introspective and concerned only with what the seller wants

To be good implies being prepared, customer-focused and so on, and not being introspective. Other things are important too:

Good selling is:

- acceptable (what customers want)
- persuasive (what sellers want)
- precisely considered

The details of exactly how it is done all matter, and there is a great deal more to it than just being polite and articulate about what is being sold. And the telephone, as we shall see, presents particular problems.

However, if selling is viewed as helping people to buy, then a customer-orientated approach must make sense. Selling becomes simply a part of the customer's decision-making process. Viewed this way, and tackled on a considered basis, it becomes entirely possible to overcome the popular, but caricatured, image of the archetypal high-pressure sales person, and to successfully obtain orders through meeting customers' needs.

In the case of selling on the telephone, the rewards of getting the approach right are considerable.

The advantages of telephone selling

Overall, the opportunities offered by telephone selling are threefold:

1 greater sales productivity
2 enhanced customer service
3 increased sales (revenue and profit)

Greater sales productivity
This describes the cost-effectiveness of selling. It links two specific factors:

1 cost
2 time.

The *cost* of visiting a customer individually and in person using a member of the field sales team is considerable. Such a cost must allow for the salary (and perhaps commission) of the sales person, the cost of travel, accommodation and a host of other costs ranging from the cost of their recruitment and training to administration and equipment such as laptop computers and mobile phones. It is not unusual for a single visit to cost hundreds of pounds.

On the other hand, a telephone call costs comparatively little. Of course, someone has to make it, and that person costs money, but the volume affects the cost too: a sales person might see only three or four people in a typical day, while on the telephone it might be possible to make 20, even 50, calls. Thus, in addition to the cost comparison, there is a time advantage. More contact is possible over time, and no time is wasted in unproductive activities such as travel. With worsening traffic conditions, a common factor worldwide, reducing travel makes a major saving.

So, telephone selling can be highly cost-effective, and a very productive marketing activity.

Enhanced customer service
What about service? Well, it is a truism that to sell successfully to anyone, they must remember you. The cost

of face-to-face visits means that frequency of contact may suffer. The telephone allows more frequent contacts, and provided it is not overdone, it can provide improved customer service. The net effect ensures we are remembered.

In fact, for many organisations, the best balance of call frequency is one that mixes face-to-face and telephone contact (and contact in writing) to create what the customer finds useful and yet what also gives the seller the best chance of tying down the business.

Though cost and productivity are both important here, it is the customer who finally dictates frequency. If contact is too frequent, then they quickly come to regard you as a time waster. Too little contact, and this is read as lack of interest and poor service.

Bear in mind that the quality of the contact matters too. Customers do not want just to chat. What is often described as a 'courtesy call', namely a call with no real purpose but to say 'Hello', quickly palls. Contacts need to have real meaning for the customer, and sales people need to consider how their contacts are regarded, and how they can be made useful. Remember that the call will always have some sort of impact on the prevailing image of the organisation which the customer has in mind.

A mix of face-to-face and telephone contacts provides the basis for a variety of contacts, all in their different ways useful to the customer, who gains something from the overall variety involved.

Increased sales

Ultimately, the success of telephone contact must be measured in sales terms. The range of ways in which telephone selling can contribute is considerable.

> ### The intentions of telephone selling
> - To provide a persuasive response to incoming enquiries
> - To initiate contact (either to create orders or to set up appointments for subsequent visits)
> - To recontact and create repeat business opportunities

The three types of call shown above are all rather different. They are reviewed in detail in the sections: Wednesday, Thursday and Friday respectively.

In addition, telephone selling has other specific advantages, summarised below.

- Increased frequency of contact
- Increased variety of contact
- An improved level of customer service
- An enhanced corporate image
- Minimising of costs
- Maximising of productivity
- Selling the range, or boosting particular parts of it
- Overall, increasing sales

It follows that telephone selling can be either a
sophisticated full-time activity (in some organisations, it is
the only sales activity) or used more selectively. Whether
you are on the telephone full time, one of a sales support
team who spends part of your time on this kind of activity,
or simply required to make the occasional sales call, with
what has been reviewed so far in mind, the following
sections will help you investigate how to get the best
results from what you do.

Creating the opportunity

Even when all goes well, selling on the telephone demands a succinct presentation. This is because realistically you are not going to find many people prepared to drop everything and talk to you at length. If you are going to make it work, and utilise just a few minutes effectively, then the responsibility for creating the possibility of a good call is yours. You cannot hope just to pick up the telephone, dial a number, and automatically have an eager buyer at the other end of the line.

A number of elements need considering or tying down in advance, so that you are actively creating the best possible circumstances for successful selling.

Creating acceptability for customers

The telephone may be ubiquitous, but it is also intrusive. There is no way of knowing what is going on at the other end as your call comes through. If the recipient has their boss towering over them demanding an explanation for a major crisis, then they will hardly be in the mood to do business with you; and many lesser situations can distract customers' attention.

There are three approaches that address this problem, any of which may help ensure a positive reception:

1 choosing the right moment
2 checking the time is convenient
3 highlighting the appropriateness of the telephone
  medium.

Choosing the right moment

There are two levels involved here. First, you can
prearrange and agree a time to call. This may be specific –
3.30 p.m. on Thursday – or less so – 'I will make sure I call
before midday.' This is clearly not possible when calling
someone you do not know for the first time, but with
others it is only a case of asking a simple question. Asking
will appear courteous to the customer, and is done to give
you a better chance of selling successfully.

Second, you can exercise some judgement about when you
telephone, not only accommodating your own schedule,
but also making an intelligent appreciation of the
customer's situation too. This may be based on definite
information: for example, if you know someone has a long
commuter journey into a big city, then it is perhaps sensible
not to call at the end of the afternoon when they are
running for a train. Or it may be simply a guess – perhaps
you think they commute. If you contact them regularly,
then this can move towards being prearranged.

Checking the time is convenient

Another approach is to actively address the problem of
acceptance early in the call. With someone you know, and
who you know wants to speak with you at some point, an
early question – 'Is this a good moment?' – is all that is
necessary. Offering to phone back (at an agreed time) will

probably be appreciated and makes it much more likely that when you do so, you will receive the attention you want.

If you do not know someone, or know them less well, then you need to judge carefully just when you should ask such a question. Too late and the conversation becomes affected if there is a problem at the customer's end. Too early and it gives them an easy excuse to opt out. So make sure you have got them interested and wanting to talk before you check whether this is the moment to do it.

It is better to make two calls, calling back as suggested, than to struggle through one that becomes difficult and gives you no chance of reaching a satisfactory conclusion.

There is one more point worth noting here.

Sometimes it may transpire that a customer is always simply unwilling, or unable, to come to the telephone. In other words, there is no convenient time. Certain retailers, with staff busy dealing with customers, are an example of this. If so, other means of communication need to be used. At the end of the day, the choice lies with the customer.

Highlighting the appropriateness of the telephone
Everyone you will ever speak to comes to the call viewing it in the context of their own experience to date. They will have a view of what logically can be done on the telephone and what cannot. In recent years, the range of what is considered possible here has extended considerably with, for example, the massive way in which financial services of all sorts, banking, insurance, pensions etc., have taken up this form of selling. Nowadays, people are more used than ever before to doing business by telephone.

But not everything is accepted in this way. Ask yourself, would you buy a new car just because someone telephoned you and described it? Not likely. But you might agree to go and test-drive it. What about a holiday or a fax machine? Possibly, but perhaps you would want to see pictures of the resort first, or have the machine demonstrated.

Assuming that your product or service lends itself to telephone selling (and recognising that some simply do not), what can you do to highlight the appropriateness for the customer of doing business on the telephone?

- Tell them how (and why) it will work
- Give them added information in other forms
- Make your intentions clear

Telling them may involve just a phrase – 'You'll find I can run through this with you and make it clear in five minutes or so' – or it may need more explanation. Added information may mean sending them a brochure ahead of the call and incorporating this into your call – 'Do you have the brochure in front of you? Just look at page 4 for a moment.' You can even fax (or e-mail) information during the call.

Making your intentions clear links to our next topic, that of forming clear objectives.

Setting and using objectives

Do not dismiss this as over-engineering the process: clear objectives are fundamental to success in any sort of selling. There is certainly more to selling on the telephone than just chatting about the product, and it really is true that, as the old maxim has it, 'If you don't know where you are going, any road will do.'

There is a much-quoted mnemonic which says objectives should be SMART:

- Specific
- Measurable
- Achievable
- Realistic
- Timed

Thus, it is not a *specific* objective to say to yourself that you will aim to sell 'as much as possible'. This is only a self-fulfilling prophecy; what you want is to conduct the sort of call that is tailored to achieving something specific.

If it is specific, it will also be *measurable*. This is important because the only way to judge success is to monitor what you intended to do against what you achieved. Such comparison is the basis for fine-tuning what you do and constantly doing better.

It is also best to focus on something *achievable*. Aim high by all means, but if your objective has no real hope of being achieved, then aiming for it will not create the right kind of call.

Making it *realistic* is important too. For example, an objective that aims to get the customer to take too big a step, or which demands a degree of description which is impossible using voice only, is doomed to failure.

The *timing* should always be involved. What do you aim to do during this call, within the next week or month, before the end of the financial year?

The advantages of clear objectives

- They help planning
- They make sure everything you say and do is well matched to your intention
- They help maintain a customer focus
- They avoid digression
- They assist with keeping control

A sales call needs directing. You cannot move purposefully forward unless you know the destination you are aiming for. Clear objectives are your destination, and the kind of call you make should be influenced throughout by the focus they bring to bear.

Flexibility
On the other hand, objectives should not act as a straitjacket. They are, or should be, more like a route map.

They not only assist you in planning a route, they also help you manage any diversions that may be necessary. Similarly, setting objectives should not blind you to the need for fall-back positions, alternative objectives if you like, that you also need to have in mind. Then, if it becomes apparent that you cannot (perhaps for reasons you could not anticipate) achieve your main goal, you can take aim again and still come away from the call with something worthwhile.

This kind of flexibility is particularly important with multi-stage selling, where it is not always possible to take an order by telephone, but where agreement can be sought to one of the other stages.

Multi-stage selling – subsidiary customer agreements

- Being sent something (e.g. literature or a sample)
- Visiting something (e.g. an exhibition or your showroom)
- Meeting technical staff
- Meeting a field sales person
- Having an individual quotation prepared
- Submitting information (on which the follow-up can be based)
- Completing a questionnaire
- Referring you to their colleague

Any of the above examples – and you may be able to think of more in your own business – if agreed represent a step being taken towards the ultimate objective: taking an order. As such, this kind of subsidiary objective is well worth keeping in mind.

Product knowledge

To sell successfully demands that you know your product
(or service, or course) well. Well means inside out, reliably,
consistently and certainly. Your knowledge must be up to
date, and anything you do not know you must be able to
find fast.

Sources of product information

- Your own knowledge
- Your workstation (brochures, factsheets etc.)
- Computer screens (if you use computer systems) –
  information is easily retrievable here
- Colleagues
- The product itself

All of these need organising and keeping up to date. So, you
must read – and note – information circulated internally.
Keep good files at your desk, from which you can easily
retrieve things. Keep computer-stored information up to
date and backed up, and remain familiar with the system.
Know which of your colleagues in the organisation knows
what to find and how to find it, or be able to transfer calls
promptly and efficiently to them. If your product is
manageable in size, then product samples can usefully sit on
your desk or nearby, acting as their own reminder.

However, it is one thing knowing about the product, but
another thing explaining and describing it.

Putting over product information
Not only do you have to be able to talk fluently about your
product, you have to be able to sum up, accurately for each

individual customer, the key aspects of it – and do so succinctly. Long rambling explanations have no place in telephone conversations with busy customers, especially if they appear ill thought through. Beware. This is an area many underestimate. It is all too easy to think 'I know my product, for goodness sake', so much so that what you say ceases to be considered and becomes routine and standardised.

Make no mistake, there is a major opportunity to impress here, and to differentiate yourself from less caring competitors. If you ring a hotel to book a room, for example, you might say: 'Can you explain the difference between a standard room and an executive room?' In this case, the answer is not for the sales person to simply quote a price difference. You might guess that one costs more than the other. What you want to know is why, and what you get for it. Certainly, giving such information is more likely to obtain a sale.

Product information must not only be clear, it must also be interestingly, enthusiastically and succinctly put over. It must also be *persuasively* put over, and that brings us to the concept of features and benefits.

Talking benefits
Here is the key that makes product description customer-orientated, and injects much of the power of persuasion a sales call needs. Customers buy benefits, not features. Let us be clear what these words mean:

Definitions
- *Benefits* are what the product or service does for, or means to, the customer
- *Features* are what it (or part of it) is

Simple enough, but the world is full of sales people talking about features when they should be talking about benefits. As an example, consider the following: customers do not buy precision drills (what they are), they buy the ability to make precision holes (what they will do). Listing features without benefits – for example, 'This model has an SFX interface' – risks the response 'So what?'

Not only do you have to understand what you sell, differentiating features from benefits, you must personalise them to each individual with whom you speak. Take a simple example. If a motorcar has a five-speed gearbox (one of its many features), then anyone selling it must describe what this means:

- better fuel economy (than a four-speed model)
- less wear and tear on the engine at high speeds
- quieter running on motorways

These are benefits. But they are only worth mentioning if it is known they correspond with the needs of a particular customer. If the sales person *knows* (perhaps having asked) that someone is concerned with economic motoring, then talking about money saved, the miles-per-gallon performance (benefit), and the five-speed gearbox (feature) as one of the reasons creating that good performance, begins to make a good case.

The use of benefits is made even more powerful if it reflects the customer's point of view, language and experience. Telling a restaurateur that a grill has a cooking surface of 800 square centimetres may be factually correct, but saying:' … this model can cook 8 steaks at the same time' and linking it to the lunchtime rush, describes a benefit. And it paints a picture that anyone in the restaurant business can visualise clearly in their mind's eye.

This is an important concept. Utilising it successfully can make the difference between a routine description and one that the customer feels is well matched to their point of view, expressed in their terms and which, by highlighting the appropriate 'reasons to buy' (benefits), is truly persuasive.

Talking benefits

- Know what you sell intimately
- Clarify the difference between features and benefits
- Emphasise, and often lead with, benefits
- Use features to underpin the case, showing how a benefit is created
- Prioritise (telling them not everything, but what is most important for them)

- Match benefits to individual customers and
  their needs
- Use language that paints a picture that customers
  will appreciate

The fundamentals

Whatever kind of telephone sales call you make, and whatever its purpose, making this kind of voice-only communication successful is dependent on the following five underlying factors:

1 the rules of telephone procedure
2 how you use your voice
3 the use of language
4 listening
5 creating a two-way dialogue.

Today we will review each of the above in turn.

The basic rules of telephone communication

Answer promptly
Anything else smacks of inefficiency. Four rings seems to be universally recommended as the maximum.

Identify yourself
It is rarely sufficient to say your name. Most often, you need a departmental or functional description as well. And a fully stated name sounds best – 'Patrick Forsyth' – rather than simply 'Patrick' or 'Forsyth' alone. Thus, something like 'Good morning, Sales Office, Sue Brown speaking' – works well.

Hold the phone correctly
Obvious perhaps, but it really does impede hearing if the handset is tucked under the chin or pushed aside as you reach for something. You must be clearly audible.

Decide who takes the call

Calls from customers should ideally always be taken at once. If it rapidly transpires that you should not deal with something (perhaps it needs someone more technically qualified), the call may need transferring – something that must always be explained and handled promptly.

Adopt an appropriate manner

This is not a question of insincerity or acting. But you may want to emphasis certain traits more with some people than with others – an efficient-sounding yet friendly (but not overfamiliar) tone with all customers, and more familiarity with those you know well. And added factors, such as urgency for someone clearly in a hurry, as appropriate.

Use signposting

Say something that tells the customer what is coming – 'Right, you want an update about the new quantity discount rates. Let me give you the overall basis, then the precise break points, and then we can see how it affects your ordering … .' This helps both parties, giving the caller the opportunity to amend the list, and giving you a list to keep in mind, or note down, to help you manage the call.

Listen carefully

The telephone may be a voice-only medium, but it is also two-way. Do not do all the talking. Make it clear you are listening by acknowledging points as the conversation proceeds and *make notes as necessary*.

Be polite

Always (even with difficult customers)! It is important to maintain reasonable courtesies, and with voice only, it can be easy to sound, say, abrupt when you are simply trying to be prompt. Take care.

Watch the pauses
If you say 'Hold on a second, I'll get the file', remember the pause seems long to the person waiting. Sometimes, it is better to suggest getting everything in front of you and phoning back. Or you can split what would otherwise seem a long pause into two, shorter, pauses by saying something like 'Right, I've got the file, I'll just turn up the details you want.'

Have the right information to hand
Many calls involve repetitive elements. You will make calls easier to handle if you anticipate what information is needed and have it to hand (and in a form that is convenient to deal with on the phone – for instance, papers in ring binders lie flat and do not need a hand to hold them open when you are already trying to hold the handset and write notes). Much information used these days may be displayed on screen from a computer system; even so, the same principle applies.

Take care with names
People are sensitive about their names. Get them right – do so early on – ask for the spelling and check how to pronounce them if necessary, and use them occasionally during the conversation (though not *too* much). It is annoying as an outside caller if you are asked your name by the switchboard, a secretary and the person who handles the call, and then, five minutes later, they say 'What was your name again?'

Always hang up last

It is fine to be the first to initiate the end of the call or to say 'Goodbye' (not 'Bye-ee', incidentally), but if you put the phone down last it avoids the customer thinking of something else and feeling they have been cut off over-hastily.

Project the right image

Your customer will not take your communication only at face value. They will read between the lines, asking themselves questions and believing that what they hear tacitly answers these. They ask: what kind of person is this? Would I like to know them? What will they be like to deal with in future? Do they sound expert? Would I accept their advice? Are they reliable? Is what is happening so good that we make a note of their name and resolve to ask for them specifically next time? Or is the projected image off-putting in some way – it is all too much trouble, it all takes a ridiculously long time, they do not seem to know or be able to decide anything?

Just because you are not visible when you speak on the telephone, it does not mean you are not sending out signals; you are. And you have some choice as to what they are. Do you want to come over as bright and efficient, or surly and unhelpful? How you act, what you say and the way you use your voice – all these influence this and are worth considering. Deploy the appropriate signs and you will feel the benefit over time.

People judge the organisation *through you*. They literally see you as personifying it. Action here thus starts with clarity of purpose. How does your organisation want to be seen? This needs spelling out, not simply in terms of 'good things' – efficient, high-quality etc. – but also in terms of values and feelings. Are you a caring, an innovative or an exceptional organisation? And if so, in what way?

You need to think about how such intentions should be reflected in the manner that comes over when you speak on the telephone, and to build in an emphasis on those things that are important in your kind of business.

Whatever rules, principles or good intentions there may be, the whole process of telephone communication is also dependent on another thing: your voice and how you use it.

Using your voice to positive effect

Few of the techniques referred to so far will work well without consideration of that most important element of telephone manner: the voice. Not only is the voice an important element, it has to act alone: by definition, telephone communication is voice-only. This makes for some difficulty. Try describing to someone how to, say, tie a necktie. You can *show* someone how, but *telling* them how is difficult if not impossible.

As with the basic rules, the details here matter. The following, in no particular order of priority, are all important:

Speak at an appropriate pace
You do not need to overdo this and slow down so that you appear to be half a-s-l-e-e-p. But pace is important. A considered pace is more likely to allow things to be made clear, and misunderstandings to be avoided. It allows the listener to keep up, particularly for example when it is clear they may be wanting to make a note: slow down especially for that.

In addition, too rapid-fire a delivery can sound glib and promote a lack of trust. It is important not to sound like a dodgy second-hand-car dealer, who will always go at a rate that precludes easy interruption.

Use inflection to enhance meaning
Inflection is what makes, for example, a question stand out at the end of a sentence, and also what gives variety and interest to the way you speak. It is important that intended inflection be noticed. *Isn't it?*

Smile
Even though a smile cannot be seen, a pleasant smile (not a fixed grin) produces a pleasant tone, and this does make for the right sound. A warm tone of voice produces a feeling that the speaker is pleasant, efficient, helpful and, most importantly, interested in the person at the other end.

There are many situations with customers when enthusiasm is important. This has to be heard; and it is about the only good thing in life that is contagious!

Add the right emphasis
It is necessary to get the emphasis right both in terms of words – '*This* is really important', or 'This is *really important*' – and in terms of the part of the message to which the listener must pay most attention. For example, if a customer struggling to note a barrage of detail coming at them over the phone then suddenly hears: 'The details don't really matter. When you come through to us next time, just quote the following reference … . This will get you through at once', they may well conclude that it would have been better if you had said that first.

Ensure clarity

It is no good sounding pleasant if what you say cannot be understood. Be clear, and be particularly careful about: names, numbers (you do not want to allow a 15-per-cent discount to be confused with 50 per cent, for instance), and sounds that can be difficult to distinguish – F's and S's for instance. Just clear, thoughtful articulation helps here.

One important detail is worth emphasising. Find ways of ensuring clarity that work. For example, a postcode ending 'BB' is worth emphasising by adding the phrase 'B for butter'.

Exercise some care if you have an accent (say, a regional accent). You have no reason to apologise for it, but you may need to bear in mind that some elements of it will not be as clear to others as they are to you. Though, having said that, some organisations favour the character that a regional accent lends to a telephone transaction which may otherwise seem impersonal.

Be positive

This is especially important when an impression of efficiency is key. Avoid saying 'possibly', 'maybe' and 'I think', when the expectation is that you should be giving definite information. (Do not waffle, however: if you do not know, say so – you can always offer to get back to people.)

Be concise

Most of the people you will speak with, in a business context, expect and appreciate your respecting their time. This means that convoluted descriptions need to be thought about in advance, and made concise and yet precise.

Be careful with the social chat. This is often liked by regular contacts, but there can be a thin line between it being a pleasure to hear you again, and you being felt to be a time waster.

Avoid jargon

Jargon is professional shorthand, and can be very useful – in its place. But you need to be sure of what another person understands and select the level of jargon to be used accordingly. Otherwise, you can find you are blinding people with science, as it were, and some – not wanting to appear foolish by asking – may allow the meaning to be diluted. For example, beware of company jargon (abbreviations of a department, process or person, perhaps), of industry jargon (technical descriptions of products and processes), and even of general phrases that contain an agreed internal definition that is not immediately apparent to an outsider, such as 'good delivery'. What is 24-hour service, other than not sufficiently well defined? You can probably think of many more examples, some close to home.

Be descriptive

A good description can add powerfully to any message. There is all the difference in the world between saying that something is 'smooth as silk' and describing it as 'sort of shiny'. Things that are inherently difficult to describe can create a powerful impact if a well-thought-out description surprises by its eloquence.

Conversely, beware of bland descriptions that impart minimal meaning. This means no company's product is 'quite nice', and that nowadays saying that something is 'user friendly', is a cliché that simply fails to differentiate it from anything else.

Use gestures
Of course, these cannot be seen. But they may make a difference to how you sound, contributing to a suitable emphasis, for instance. Be careful, however: you have to hang onto the phone and not knock everything off the desk!

Adopt the right tone
In most circumstances, you want to be friendly without being flippant. You always want to sound courteous, and also you want to tailor your style to the circumstance, consciously deciding whether to produce a note of respect, a feeling of attention to detail or whatever. Getting this right is what produces a good telephone 'handshake' feeling.

Be yourself
Sound like yourself. And certainly avoid adopting a separate, contrived 'telephone voice'; it does not tend to work and is difficult to sustain.

All these voice factors are things that can be consciously varied. Some – for example, clarity – may need experiment, rehearsal and practice. But together they combine to produce a satisfactory manner. The effect is cumulative, and this works both ways. It means that any shortfalls begin to add up, eventually diluting the overall power of what is done. Equally, the better you work in all these areas, the more the effects combine to create a satisfactory overall impression and style.

How your voice sounds goes logically with the way you use language, so we turn next to a few points under this heading.

The use of language

Several of the points above touch on language as much as voice – descriptiveness, for one. The point has also already been made that you should be yourself. So avoid 'gobbledegook'. A few examples are sufficient to make the point. Do not say:

- at this moment in time (when you mean *now*)
- due to the fact that (*because*)
- I am inclined to the view that (*I think*)

and do not overdo the 'we' – who is this corporate 'we', for goodness sake? Make things personal: 'I will ensure that' sounds totally committed. In addition, refer to people by name: 'Mary Brown, in Accounts, will … ' is much better than 'someone'.

Although grammatical perfection is not essential in conversation, it is good to avoid those things that irritate – for example, adding several additional superlatives to the word unique; nothing can be 'very unique', and such language risks annoying, and therefore can detract from any good sense being talked.

Watch also for habits which can introduce an annoying or incorrect note: for example, ending every other sentence with 'right' or 'okay', or starting with a superfluous use of 'Basically'.

However well you speak and however well you get your point over, no telephone conversation can be a monologue. You need to generate feedback, and the first step to this is, not unnaturally, to listen. There is an old saying that people have two ears and one mouth for a good reason, and certainly we should always remember that listening is just as important as speaking.

Listening

Good communication demands good listening skills, and this is especially vital on the telephone when there are few other signs. Not only does it give you more information, other people like it. But you need to work at it. The following points describe how to make listening an active process. You must:

- *want to listen:* this is easy once you take on board how useful it is;
- *sound like a good listener:* this comes through both in language – 'Tell me about …' and in tone;
- *strive to understand:* you need to read between the lines, not simply listen to the words (experience helps here);
- *react:* let people know you are listening by making small acknowledging comments – 'Right', 'Okay', 'Go on';
- *stop talking:* remember, you cannot talk and listen at the same time, nor is it polite to try to do so;
- *use empathy:* put yourself in other peoples' shoes and make sure you appreciate their point of view;

- *check:* always check as you go along. Do not guess, and if you are not sure what is meant, ask, sooner rather than later;
- *concentrate:* do not let anything distract you (even in a busy office);
- *note key points:* always have paper and pencil in front of you when you talk on the telephone, and make notes: sometimes, points that are key do not become apparent until later, and you do not want to keep saying, 'What was it you said about … ?';
- *not let your mind wander:* it is easy to find you are so busy trying to decide what to say next (for instance, how to rebut something) that you lose your way in listening.

Good listening skills are a sound foundation for any sort of communication, and on the telephone are always going to add to the likelihood of success.

Creating a dialogue

Two-way communication does not just demand talking one at a time and listening while others speak. Creating a dialogue is something you need to actively work at.

Dialogue involves:

- talking *with* people rather than *at* them
- maintaining a two-way flow
- not jumping to conclusions
- sounding well organised

Talk with *people not* at *them*
It may help to form a mental picture of the person at the other end. Certainly, treating them like a disembodied voice does not create the right impact.

Maintain a two-way flow
Do not interrupt. Make sure, if they are talking at some length, that they are sure you are still there and listening – 'Right ...' – and flag what you are going to do to make your intentions clear: 'Good. I have those details. Now perhaps I can just set out ... '.

Do not jump to conclusions
For whatever reasons. It may be that you do know what is coming, but if you make unwarranted assumptions, it can cause problems.

Give the feeling of things being well handled
The dialogue should not just flow, it should actively appear to deal with things as necessary. The whole manner and structure needs to get to the point and clearly be doing whatever is necessary to sort something out.

One last thought at this stage: always keep firmly in mind what customers are looking for from outside contacts. Something that fits their perception and expectation of how a thing should be done will stand a better chance of success than something that ignores their feelings.

BUT WHATEVER YOU DO, DON'T MENTION "MOTHER-IN-LAW" OR HIS LAST BUSINESS VENTURE

Meet peoples' expectations

- Sound interested in talking to them
- Let them have their say
- Make it clear you are really listening
- Respect their time: keep things succinct
- Be businesslike and efficient

If you are also going to make a call persuasive, then all
these factors are important.

*Good, clear, customer-orientated communication that recognises
the inherent difficulties of voice-only communication and makes
it as easy and satisfying as possible for the customer, is the
soundest basis for successful selling.*

Handling incoming calls

A great deal of time, effort and money is likely to be spent in encouraging prospective customers to contact your organisation. When they do call, everything about their contact must go well. Such a call represents a range of opportunities, from obtaining an immediate order to securing and extending business for the future.

Today, we shall look at how to make this kind of incoming call truly sales orientated.

Your voice, as was reviewed in Tuesday's section, is a major asset. But it is not sufficient just to be pleasant and well spoken; if it is a sales opportunity, then you need to handle the whole thing in a way that makes it truly persuasive.

Even though an incoming call may seem to need a reactive approach, which to a degree it does, it also demands that you take ownership of the call and make it work for you. Thus, it needs planning.

The advantages of planning

- It overcomes any nervousness
- It assists the ability to think quickly
- It ensures clear objectives are set
- It prevents inappropriate digression (or being sidetracked) during the call
- It makes the call customer-focused
- It helps measure success and foster improvement

Planning need not be elaborate. It is no more than the simple expedient of 'engaging the brain before the mouth'.

But it should put you in a position to handle most of the typical situations that occur without floundering. There is little room for long pauses and extended thought once you take a call. Planning (and practice) make perfect.

You do not need to adopt a scripted or 'parrot-like' approach (something customers can spot at once and do not like). Rather, you should respond to the customer, yet control the direction of the call towards a specific objective. It may help to think of this graphically: rather as the helmsman of a yacht, proceeding across open sea and subject to the impact of wind and tide, might take a number of courses, though their knowledge of the clear position of their chosen destination will allow a route to be selected that sees the boat make its chosen landfall.

Sound preparation

- Have product literature and customer information to hand
- Have in mind the kind of call you would, ideally, like to occur
- Have appropriate first responses ready
- Think through appropriate product descriptions
- Note, and be ready to anticipate, typical objections
- Have in mind, or on a checklist, the kind of questions you want to ask
- Be clear where you are going and how the call should end

With this thought in mind, you can now consider the progression of the stages of the enquiry-handling call and how you can direct it to make it go the way you want.

The intention here is clear: conduct the call in the way you want (to make it persuasive), yet make it a call the customer finds they like too (because it meets their expectations).

There are several stages:

First response

If calls come to you through a switchboard, then you must link to what is said there, avoiding repetition or gaps in information. For example, do not repeat the organisation's name if that has just been stated, or ask what theirs is – again!

The role of the first response

- To welcome the customer and put them at ease
- To make it clear you are there to help
- To create a feeling of efficiency and helpfulness

If, at the end of the first few seconds of the call, a customer is saying to themselves 'This seems a good start', and is encouraged to feel optimistic about the remainder of the call being helpful for them, then you are over the first hurdle.

So, include an appropriate greeting – 'Good morning' – make clear your name and role, ask the customer's name (and check other details, getting them straight and out of the way early on – the correct spelling of their name, what company they work for and in what capacity, their account number (for existing customers) – as necessary), and move promptly on.

Equipment must help not hinder

So many people answering incoming calls now sit at computer screens that this situation demands a specific note of advice. Computers are not, yet, synonymous with efficiency, and it is good practice to:

- explain what you are doing as you do it (' ... If you give me your postcode first, I can enter that and call up your address in a moment ... . ')
- refer to how long action on systems will take, to explain any delay that might be noticed
- comment on how this helps the customer ('... If I do this, it will save you having to dictate all the details ... .')

It is always worth being careful about this; the advantages to you are obvious, but a customer may wonder what it is all about, or actively distrust it.

Finding out what they want

This stage may consist of no more than listening. But always:

- listen *very carefully* and
- *make notes* as you go

Customers understandably find it very annoying if they have to repeat things, or if a call is handled in a way that makes it obvious that something they said is being ignored.

Being able to get to the nub of the matter accurately and quickly is impressive. Doubly so as frankly the prevailing standards of many organisations leave something to be desired. Do not underestimate the power of simply doing what you may regard as the basics really well.

This stage demands:

Identifying enquirers' needs

- Find out exactly who they are
- Listen to exactly what they want
- Clarify the requirement if necessary
- Ask questions to focus the reply
- Volunteer information creatively

If you know who they are (name, job function etc.), where they are from (the kind of organisation and what it does), *exactly* what the need or problem is and why that is so, then everything else you say can be *individually directed*. Customers like to be treated like individuals (for the very good reason that that is what they are!), and dislike being dealt with in a way that appears standardised.

Tailoring what you say to each customer is an important part of getting their attention and beginning to persuade them.

Responding to their requirement

Your description of what you offer must now be:

- *appropriate*. It must be appropriate for them and for you, with your not embarking on a complete technical rundown if they simply want a brief overview and a brochure in the post. But do not fail to give a necessary level of detail and, from your point of view, to take them further towards your objectives if you can. They may be persuaded that the brochure is unnecessary and proceed straight to an order.

- *understandable*. Clarity is a powerful ally of persuasion. People are impressed by crisp, clear descriptions that allow them to understand the first time and to do so promptly. This is especially true if they anticipate difficulty (or have just been talking to a competitor who blinded them with science), and clarity surprises.

  If the descriptions you use (probably repetitively) become an unthinking habit, then they may suffer as a result. For example, it is easy to start to abbreviate something until it no longer does the job you originally intended. It is well worth regularly thinking through how you describe things to make sure it will not confuse in any way.

- *attractive*. This is where the concept of talking benefits (dealt with in Monday's section) is so vital. Tell people what your product or service will *do* for them, and show them what it can *mean* for them, and they are much more likely to buy.

  Price should be mentioned under this heading. Always link the price to benefits: ' ... That's the total cost, and it includes delivery and installation. It's good value given the way it will simplify your ... .' By all means justify price, remembering it is value for money that people are ultimately concerned about, but never apologise for it. Your attitude should be one of saying: 'Yes it is (so much) and worth every bit of it.' Cheapness is rarely a benefit. Quality, which creates higher prices, is often linked to money.

- *credible*. Bear in mind that customers know that you are selling. They expect you to take the view that whatever you are selling is good, whether it is or not. So, any sales-orientated description needs to build in credibility.

This means adding something to the case that is not just your own opinion. Tell people what independent standards your product meets, what tests it has passed, who speaks well of it, how many it has sold etc. – anything that reinforces your case by adding outside opinion. This is especially effective if there is real measurement involved: the Automobile Association's tested figure giving the miles per gallon achieved by a particular car, would be a good example.

In addition:

Overcoming objections
Expect objections. They are a natural part of the customer's task of weighing something up and assessing what is good, and less good, about it. Sometimes, objections will be erroneous: customers simply misunderstand something or make assumptions. In this case, it may be comparatively easy to change their view, though do not give the impression that they should have known better. It is better to respond along the lines of 'Perhaps I did not make that completely clear. Actually, it is … ' rather than 'No, that's not right. Can't you see … '.

No product is perfect, however, and it may be that yours does have certain disadvantages. Here the job is to rebalance the pluses and minuses, minimising the impact of the objection, and linking what you say to a description that maximises the other side of the balance: '… Of course, four weeks' delivery does delay things a little, but once it arrives you can have it up and running that day, and immediately see savings resulting.'

Ask for a commitment

Whatever your objective, you need to ask for the commitment you want. If you want an order, or for the customer to take some other action first – test a sample perhaps – then you must take responsibility for initiating the 'close'. It is easy to miss this stage. Checking that all is well – 'Does that give you all the information you need at this stage?' – can leave the door open for the customer to say thank you and goodbye. The conversation is terminated before you can complete what you set out to do.

How you close – with a question: 'Can I get that dispatched this week?', an assumptive statement: 'Right, we seem to be agreed. Let me see to the documentation and you can have delivery this week', or an alternative: 'Would you like 50 or 100?' – is almost less important than being sure that you do actually close, and do so firmly.

Closing can never make people order. It is everything else
that has been done during a call that does that. But it can
act to prompt a decision and the taking of action – now.
This is a key factor in any kind of sales call, and it needs to
be borne in mind throughout every aspect of the process.

Last but not least
When you have obtained the commitment you want, or
reached a satisfactory conclusion, then: stop.

Signing off

- Always thank the customer (even if you do not have
  their agreement to anything)
- Confirm any follow-up action clearly
- Be sure that both parties have noted all the
  information they need
- Build goodwill with positive statements
- Ring off; fast but last

This ensures that all the loose ends are tied up, for example
that the customer has any reference numbers or peoples'
names they may need. It strikes a concluding note of
efficiency and avoids wasting their time (or allowing them
to think better of things: if the call moves into lengthy final
chatter, it is easy to find them saying something like: 'You
know, thinking about what we agreed, I am not sure ...').

Now, some final hints to round off today's review of
responsive calls:

Hints for successful enquiry handling

- Plan the call, but remain quick on your feet
- Appear to be dealing with every call as a unique case
- Always have all the information you need to hand
- Explore the customer's need with questions
- Make notes as the call progresses
- Offer alternatives, if necessary
- Always see and describe the product from the customer's point of view
- Listen to objections – never argue – and deal with them by rebalancing
- Repeat important details
- Keep control, and close positively

Taking the initiative

Today, we review what is usually known as 'cold calling'.
This is calls made to people with whom there has been no
prior contact, aiming either to obtain immediate orders or to
set things up for the future. (Calls made specifically to make
an appointment for a sales person to call are dealt with in
the next section.) There are two key stages to cold contact:

1 getting through to the right person
2 handling the subsequent call.

1 Getting through to the right person

Clearly, to get through to the right person, you need to
know who that is. And you may not know in advance.
Finding out may come from prior research (which may be
best) but can also be done at the start of the call. If the
latter, then you just need to dial and ask 'May I have the
name of your Training Manager?' If the switchboard
operator tells you, then you can go on to ask to speak to
them. If they interrogate you about who is calling and why,
never tell lies (you are *not* 'just doing some research', for
example). Just say your name, add your job position and
company if you are asked and take your time. Switchboards
tend to be busy, so as other calls come in they will often give
you the information you want in order to terminate the call.

Then, you can either ask to be put through, or, if it is clear
to them you are a sales person and there is resistance, it
may be better to thank them for the information, hang up

and try again later – next time simply asking for the name you have been given.

Even when you have the right name, you may still have difficulty getting through. If they are not there, ask when is a good time to catch them. You will not always get a useful answer but often you will, and making a practice of asking is going to make at least some such calls easier.

Getting through the 'gatekeepers'
Gatekeepers are all those people – secretaries, assistants and others – who interpose between you and the people with whom you really want to speak.

Communicating with gatekeepers

- Never antagonise them
- Regard them as a source of information
- Regard them as potential allies
- Treat them with respect

Answer all their questions – about who you are, what organisation you represent, what you want – though do not say: 'I want to sell him some ... '. Talk about what is in it for them: 'I want to ask her a bit about your communications systems. We make a range of products that might well help your organisation improve its efficiency.' Make this kind of comment as specific to your own business area as you can.

If whoever you want is not there, request their help:

- 'When will they next be in the office?'
- 'How long is their meeting likely to last?'
- 'When is a good time to make contact?'

It is particularly useful to be able to quote answers to such questions next time you call, perhaps being able to say to a switchboard operator: 'I arranged to call Mr Forsyth this afternoon.'

Two further ideas that may help are:

1 to use full names. Asking to speak to John Smith, rather than Mr Smith, often seems to allow others to infer that you know them;
2 to check with the intermediary that you are, in fact, trying to contact the right person. A secretary might well say that they handle all purchases of something themselves, and you can then simply continue the conversation with them (or contact whoever else they explain is involved).

If all else fails and you persistently cannot get past a gatekeeper, then go round them. Try telephoning again at lunchtime. Even secretaries have to eat. And most managers have at least a short period during the day when they are answering the telephone themselves.

Finally, remember that you may well speak to a particular gatekeeper again. A first contact should begin a relationship. If they form a positive impression of you as reasonable, pleasant and, above all, likely to be helpful to them and their organisation, then future contacts will be no problem.

Regard gatekeepers as allies – and get them to regard you in the same light.

2 Handling the call itself

All the factors described in Wednesday's section about describing the product apply here. Certain factors are especially important with cold calls, and we will concentrate here on these.

Key factors in handling cold calls
- Getting the first few moments right
- Establishing interest
- Creating a feeling of worth
- Overcoming objections

The clichés abound – e.g. 'You only get one chance to make a good first impression' – but they are true. Almost certainly, if you are not making some progress in the first couple of minutes, you never will. Consider very carefully how you use them.

First impressions last
Assume the worst. The person you call is most likely to feel they do not know you, do not want to speak to you and regard you as one more interruption in a busy day. What might change their mind? Of course, if they are certainly

SO IMPRESSED WAS I BY YOUR MARVELLOUS RANGE OF PRODUCTS THAT I THOUGHT YOU ALONE SHOULD BE OFFERED...

never in the market for your kind of product, then nothing may change their mind. Some calls may be aborted early on to the advantage of both parties. But if they are potential buyers, see how you can differentiate yourself from the many unsuitable or unprofessional people who call them. There are several ways to do this:

Differentiating yourself in the early stages

- Give evidence of research, and appear to have targeted them accurately
- Establish familiar ground with them quickly
- Appear at pains to focus on their situation

Thus, if you show that you know something about them, what the organisation does, how your product might fit in, why it seems appropriate to talk to this particular person about it, this will begin to establish your credentials.

The common alternative of a long, 'Interrupt me if you dare while I tell you what I *want*' introduction quickly switches people off.

Establishing interest

A bridge must quickly be constructed between what interests the customer and what is important to you. As well as the description begun early on, you need to ask questions to make the link and get into the detail of what might help them.

This is best illustrated by a simple example. Imagine a travel agent (TA) talking to an export manager (ExM):

TA: 'What parts of the world are your priorities at present?'

ExM: 'The Middle East is next for major investigation, but Germany is the short-term priority.'

TA: 'Why is that?'

ExM: 'Well, we're exhibiting at a trade fair in Germany soon. That will tie up staff and use up a good deal of our budget. So what we want to do in the Middle East must wait.'

TA: 'What sort of problems might a delay cause?'

ExM: 'Well, the time it takes to set things up in the Middle East is longer anyway, so it could affect the results for this financial year.'

TA: 'Have you ever thought of moving one of your people on to the Middle East from Germany?'

ExM: 'No. Why?'

TA: 'I think I could show you some real savings over making two separate trips, and it would save time. Maybe such a trip would let you get more under way this year.'

ExM: 'Could be, I suppose. Tell me ... '.

Here, interest is generated through questions and information. The questions are open, and topics are pursued, digging for information, until something is produced that actively helps the sales presentation to be made. The focus is on the customer's needs, and the conversation is beginning to develop along lines they want to pursue. Interest is always fragile, however, and will need to be maintained, but this call is on the right tracks.

Creating a feeling of worth

The example call on page 61 is not only establishing interest, it is also creating worth. The customer is being offered things that are valuable in their terms: financial savings to make the budget go further and allow more to be achieved in the current financial year, and a possible saving on time away from home and office. This is very different from offering standard advantages off a checklist.

Because the factors mentioned could only have come from the conversation (rather than being standard-sounding offerings), they find more favour with the customer. They feel they are being treated as an individual and that trouble is being taken to discover what is right for them.

Overcoming objections

Objections can occur at any time during any call. They are a natural part of the buying process and represent a positive opportunity to find out more and take things further.

A positive response to objections

- Expect them and be prepared for them
- Acknowledge them to show you respect them
- Do not argue or dismiss them lightly
- Give what appears a considered response
- Make your answer individual

Some objections are classic, and you can have suitable replies ready:

- *'You're just trying to sell me something.'*
  'No, it is too early for that. First, we must see whether your situation makes the kind of benefits our product offers useful or not. May I just ask a couple of brief questions ... ?'

- *'It's a waste of time.'*
  'If I can help you increase productivity even a little,
  wouldn't that be time well spent? Let me ask ... .'

- *'Just give me a quick description and tell me what it costs.'*
  I won't keep you any longer than necessary, but I don't want
  to waste time describing anything unless I know enough
  about your situation to see that it might be useful ... .'

Other objections are just a smoke screen:

- *'I'm not interested.'* (Or do they need more information
  before they can tell?)
- *'Your price is too high.'* (Or do they not yet see the
  relevance of the offer?)
- *'Your product/company is no good.'* (In what way? Why
  do they say this?)

All such objections provide opportunities to ask further
questions, redirect the conversation or go back to an
earlier point.

Of course, you do not win them all, particularly with cold
calls. The best possible strike rate could be low. But correct
and positive handling of objections will keep the average up.

In all cases, your response should:

- *accept* the prospect's point of view without necessarily
  agreeing with it. An acknowledgement that starts with a
  'yes' can sound better than a denial: 'Yes, that is
  sometimes a problem, certainly something to consider. In
  this case, though, ... ';
- *minimise* or correct the point of view by repeating the
  objection in your own words, perhaps in the form of a
  question, and playing down its real or perceived impact;

- *compensate* by referring to one or more definite advantages which outweigh the (small) disadvantage.

So, if you still feel apt to say: 'But objections make selling really difficult', a final example might be the reply: 'Well, it may seem so, and they certainly do not make it any easier. But they are opportunities too, and handled right they can remove a doubt from someone's mind and impress by the way that is done.'

The balanced call

Cold calls do not demand some magic ingredient – there is no one thing that can guarantee their success. They work well only when all that goes on in them works well together.

The success of cold calls is made more likely if they:

- are well targeted
- have clear objectives
- are well planned, yet flexible
- are customer focused   *FIND OUT ABOUT THEIR Co.*
  WHAT THEY DO.

To conclude our consideration of this kind of call, each of the above points is commented on, briefly, in turn:

Well targeted
Research is vital. You must not simply pick names out of a
hat, or a directory, at random. If you have a clear idea of the
kind of contact who is most likely to buy (which may need
no more than a look at who has bought in the past), then you
can select targets that meet the brief: the right kind of person,
organisation, situation, size etc. Not least, those selected
must have not just an interest but also a real need, the
authority to take action and, last but not least, the money to
pay (it is not a sale until the money is in the bank!).

Well-chosen and well-qualified prospects are the basis for
making calls with a good chance of success.

Clear objectives
There may be various possible positive outcomes: an order,
sending literature – whatever. You need these clearly in
mind throughout the call. Selling is not just 'talking about
the product,' it is matching what you offer to customer
needs and selecting and moving towards objectives likely
to work for both parties. After all, only by satisfying
customers' needs can you encourage them to buy again.

Planned, yet flexible
All sales calls should be planned. Some of what you say
may even need to come close to a script. If it is important to
get an element of, say, a product description exactly right –
and it may well be – then have it noted down. Certainly,
notes that remind you how one thing leads to another,
written in checklist style, are invaluable.

But it is practically impossible just to read what you want
to say verbatim and make it sound natural, much less make

it sound personalised to the individual. Beware taking preparation – and scripting – too far in this direction.

Customer focused
This is an overriding factor. Everything done and said must come over as concern for the customer. Any evidence of the call just being a request for 'what the sales person wants' is likely to scupper any chance of success.

These are the special considerations with cold calls. In addition, all the other factors mentioned to date, from use of your voice to a clear product description and a firm closing statement, are important too.

So is a positive attitude. The number of rejections of cold calls can be high, even when they are well made. But everything you have reviewed here can act together to strengthen what you do and create a sufficient level of success to make cold calls well worthwhile.

Developing repeat business

There is an old saying that: 'The selling starts when the customer says "Yes"'. Here, on the penultimate day, we consider the ongoing selling that can be done on the telephone to prompt repeat orders and extend the scale of the business. As it is true to say that it is usually easier to sell more to existing customers than to sell to new ones, this is an area well worth consideration.

First, let us consider timing. How long do you leave it before recontacting someone who has bought in the past? There is no one answer to this. A small trial order may need following up in a matter of days. Other kinds of business may have the potential for repeat ordering on a much longer lead time.

What is important is that this be considered *individually*, and that follow-up intentions be linked to a system that prompts action at a particular, well-chosen, time. It matters less how this is done (systems can range from a simple card index to a sophisticated computer customer-record system that includes a prompting facility) than that it is done consistently. It is otherwise very easy to find that other priorities put the matter out of mind. The danger is then that the moment passes, and it becomes more and more difficult to follow up once the ideal timing has passed.

Being persistent

Keeping in touch is vital, and this applies equally, if not more so, when the customer is reluctant to pursue matters. Most people in selling will know the feeling. You telephone, and they are busy – out of town, in a meeting, or whatever. This occurs several times in a row. Paranoia quickly sets in, you become convinced they are avoiding you and you cease to make contact. Leave it too long and it becomes impossible to think of a convincing way of restarting a dialogue.

This kind of non-action occurs all too easily, yet one of the easiest, most cost-effective, ways of increasing sales is simply to ensure this does not happen. You must be persistent. Just one more call can crack the logjam and bring in more business.

The possible methods of ongoing contact may need to be varied. This is important. Just because you sit at a workstation designed primarily for telephone contact does not mean customers do not like, and will not respond to, other methods of approach.

Keeping in touch

- Telephone
- Letters
- Faxes
- E-mail

Every method has a role to play, and in combination they can be powerful. An abortive telephone call followed by a letter or fax sets the scene for the next contact. Such an approach shows interest and commitment. Eventually, if people are being evasive, they will either tell you that your continued contact is a waste of time, or respond when the time is favourable for them. Some of the people constantly 'in a meeting' really are. They *are* interested, but *they* will

pick the time. You may want to sell today, but why realistically should they want to buy today? Ultimately, it is the customer's timescale that dictates events.

In the kind of business where orders are occasional (once or twice a year, say, rather than every week or month), you can aim to agree to a particular level of regularity.

Agreeing the timing

In this case, you need first to agree to the principle of telephone contact. After all, if you are calling a retailer, for example, their being out of stock of a product may be losing them sales. A regular telephone call, perhaps between the face-to-face visits of the field sales staff, may well be in everybody's interest. The first follow-up call may do no more than agree what will be done in future. But this is an important step, allowing subsequent calls to be gone into automatically with the agreement of the customer.

Setting up the level of regularity

- Spell out to them how regular calls will help them
- Suggest, discuss and agree to the frequency level: every other Thursday, or whatever
- Ask what the best time is for them (day of the week, time of day etc.)
- Promise to call only at that time
- Suggest and agree to what both parties need to hand when the call takes place (e.g. an up-to-date stock position)
- Give them an honest estimate of how long such a call will take
- Link to what will be done afterwards (e.g. how confirmation of any order will be handled)
- Then stick to what is agreed (discussing and agreeing any future changes before building them into the way you work)

Approaching things along these lines, you can create a way of working that works for both parties. Customers will be expecting your calls, and may even look forward to them. Calls can get straight down to business and will take less time. Business obtained is maximised, and everyone is happy. But how exactly do you handle the calls themselves?

Making the call

Once set up, regular calls should be straightforward in some senses, but they still benefit from a systematic approach.

Factors to include in repeat business calls

- Be prepared, and let it show
- Be friendly
- Initiate the business of the call and aim to close
- Spell out the administrative detail
- Sign off appropriately

Consider a little about each of these:

Be prepared
Always have everything you need to hand, and make sure any facts and figures are up to date. Because the customer knows you have had time to get organised, they will tend to be unforgiving of any inefficiency. Remember they are busy, and let your concern for their time show.

Be friendly
You will quickly build up a relationship through such calls, even with people you have never met. This can be pleasant for both parties, and a little social chit chat may act to

smooth the way for the business of the call that follows. But do not overdo it. There is a thin line between being welcome and becoming seen as a time waster. Remember, you cannot see what is happening at the other end, and so you will be unaware, unless you check, how convenient it is to extend the call.

Initiate the business of the call
See it as your role to direct the call. You should signpost what needs to be done – 'Right, what we need to do is go through those stock figures and see what lines need replenishing. Then there is a new promotion I would like to tell you about ...' – making it easy for the customer. Then you can direct the call through to the close, asking for a specific order or commitment.

Spell out the administrative detail
Be sure to be completely clear about action that is agreed.
Spell out all details – what is ordered, rates, discounts,
delivery times etc. – so that there can be no prospect of
misunderstanding.

Getting this right is good for your image and helps
persuade the customer to keep the arrangement going.

Signing off
The best way to end, after sorting the details, is with a link
to the next call. This can be done, in part, just to double-
check convenience – 'I'll speak to you again on Friday
week; that's the 15th. Is 3.00 p.m. still the best time?' But it
can also serve to flag future intention – 'If I can keep you
just a few minutes longer next time, I will have the details
of the new product launch I mentioned ... .' – and to set
things up for an effective call next time.

If the above makes such calls seem routine, then it is
because they should be. But the customer will only make
time for them as long as they find them useful, so they
must be considered regularly, kept fresh and made
interesting. Getting into a rut with them makes it likely that
customers will gradually see them as less useful.

The routine aspects of such calls can bring in good
business. The merits of existing products may need little
real selling. If, for example, you sell office supplies, then
once a laser printer has been sold, the job of selling paper
and replacement toner cartridges may demand no great
power of persuasion. There are, however, other
opportunities to extend the sale.

Telephone selling should always be on the look-out for new opportunities.

> *Spotting opportunities by:*
> * asking questions
> * making links between different products/services in the range

Asking questions

The routine call should never become so prescribed that it ceases to explore the customer's situation. Nothing remains the same for ever, after all. If you are calling regularly, you do not need massive extra time and a barrage of questions like the Spanish Inquisition. Just one or two in a call may suffice. And if you get onto something interesting, more can follow; indeed, you may identify something the customer wants to explain to you and is prepared to take more time over.

The best route is again through open questions, namely those that cannot be answered 'yes' or 'no', and which typically start with words like 'What', 'Why', 'Where', 'How', 'Who' and 'When'. Or with a phrase like 'Tell me about ... ', or, when pursuing a point, with a phrase like 'Tell me more about ... ' as you dig for information.

All sorts of factors may reveal an opportunity: the customer's business increasing, overseas markets opening up, a new product being launched, one of their staff leaving (where are they going, and who is taking over? You may end up with two customers rather than one as a result of such a change). Each business lends itself to different approaches, and these need to be considered in advance so that questions can be ready. Then, any new circumstance may put you back into the mode of selling something new and take the call away from its routine of repeat-order gathering.

Making links

This involves a simple, classic and effective technique referred to by some as 'gin and tonic selling' (because if you go into an off-licence and ask for a bottle of gin, the simplest and most sales-orientated response will be to say 'How many mixers do you want?'). This clearly involves both finding the links and then introducing them. On the telephone, you have to be quick on your feet, as it were, because time is short. It follows that you must have all possible links in mind (or perhaps on some sort of checklist) before you make a call if you are to spot opportunities to introduce links and thus create the possibility of obtaining additional business.

... AND WHAT BATH FITTING WOULD BE COMPLETE WITHOUT...

It is possible to think of many examples of links:

- strawberries and cream
- management books and tapes or training courses
- laser printers and paper, toners etc.
- holidays and travel insurance
- a pension and other investments
- a birthday present, wrapping paper and card

The above give the flavour of the idea and may prompt you to think of others – preferably a comprehensive list – in your own business. This will allow you to proceed naturally from the mention of one thing to the introduction of another – 'If you need paper for the laser printer, some of that may be used in producing reports. What kind of binding system do you use for them?' Such an approach combines the use of a question with the making of a link, and might in this case lead on to the selling of more supplies – or even, in this example, to the selling of a binding machine.

The conclusion

Establishing routine repeat-order-gathering calls, and making them truly useful for customers, can create an additional flow of cost-effectively obtained business. Regarding them creatively, exploring other possibilities and creating new opportunities as you do so can expand the business done through such calls still more.

Again, all that is necessary is a systematic approach and attention to detail in the manner in which calls are conducted.

Working with the field sales team

It's the end of the week. Now, on the last day, you can
consider an additional skill that will allow you to
significantly increase your contribution to the effectiveness
of the field sales team in terms of:

- its individual productivity, and
- the sales result it can produce

Much of what has been dealt with in previous sections can
be initiated by the individual – that's you – and the sales
results that accrue can also, very largely, be laid at the
individual's door.

Here, you review an area where the objective is for you not to
take orders directly but, equally importantly, to obtain
commitment from the customer to their taking a tangible step
towards buying: to obtain agreement to meet a sales person.
In multi-step sales processes where an order is dependent on
several stages (a meeting, a proposal, a demonstration or
presentation or whatever), this is a vital step.

Before going on to look at just *how best* you can set up an
appointment, you can usefully consider briefly just how
much doing so positively affects the overall sales situation.

Appointment fixing is beneficial in:

- improving sales productivity
- increasing sales results

Both deserve a word more:

Improving sales productivity

Like all of us, field sales people have only limited time. The way they organise their time directly affects their sales success: simplistically, the more sales meetings they have, the more orders they are likely to obtain. They must decide:

- whom to see
- how many meetings they can fit in (without the quality of those meetings suffering)
- how often they see those who need follow-up or become regular customers

By setting up appointments, you can help increase the number of meetings they will hold. Instead of spending time on the telephone or seeing prospects of lesser potential, much of their time will be spent seeing qualified prospects – those who have expressed sufficient interest to agree to see them.

Improving sales effectiveness

Even when an appointment is set, the sales meeting itself must be well handled. The impression given if your first approach is appropriate and efficient can boost the prospect's perceptions of the whole organisation. Thus, you can make the subsequent meeting just a little easier to run, and more likely to produce results.

In addition, information you obtain during the telephone call will help the sales person focus the way they handle things more accurately – again increasing the chances of success.

Appointment setting is therefore very worthwhile. It can be undertaken by the sales person themselves or by a support-staff colleague; someone like you for instance! To keep the description specific, we will assume here that you are the one making the call (though for a field sales person the principles are very similar).

Setting up for success

The following tips will help you review the process chronologically. Information is power, it is said, and the first consideration is one of information. Whomever you are calling (it may be someone who has responded to an advertisement or mail shot, or simply a cold call), think about what you should have to hand. You need to consider:

> *Your information requirements:*
>
> * customer information
> * diary information
> * additional miscellaneous information (e.g. about the product or service)

You must have to hand all the customer information available to date, including a note of what business they are in (which with a cold call you may need to look up) and any 'hints' (such as a note of how to pronounce a name) that may aid the making of the call.

You also need specific diary information enabling an appointment to be made (especially if this means liaising with a sales person who will make the visit).

In addition, a checklist of any information you will try to obtain – others' products being used by the customer, their preferences, the size of their company and so on – is helpful.

Then you dial.

Making the call

Throughout the call, all the techniques about telephone manner reviewed in Tuesday's section should be borne in mind. The first job is to get through to the right person (this was dealt with in the section on approaching new customers on Thursday, and may be worth turning back to).

Once through, a structured approach gives you the best chance of success. 'Structured' means thought out, and implies a logical order in which to deal with matters. It does *not* imply a *scripted* or unthinking approach which precludes flexibility. You never know how people will react, what difficulties may be put in your way or what opportunities may appear, and you must always remain able to fine-tune what you do throughout the call.

Seven key stages
First things first. The starting point, covered by the following first three points, is how you open the conversation:

1 A greeting
Greetings should be clear, short, sharp, simple and to the point. It may be no more than 'Good morning', and can link to any check you need to make – 'Is that Sue Robertson?'.

2 Identification
Announce yourself clearly and confidently. People are often bad at retaining names, so some repetition is appropriate: 'My name is Forsyth, Patrick Forsyth, from Touchstone Training & Consultancy.' Allow for any response, but aim to move quickly on.

3 Quote reasons for calling
Remember that they are not interested in your point of view (which is ultimately to get some business from them). Your reason for calling must be customer orientated (answering their question of 'What's in it for me?'). You must talk benefits and should explain *why* you are seeking to arrange an *appointment*. The job is *not* to

comprehensively sell the product or service at this stage (after all, realistically, how long will they give you?).

Mentioning the purpose of the meeting will help you, as well as describing something the customer will see, touch, try out or have demonstrated at the meeting; ideally something that can *only* take place at a meeting (which helps stop them saying: 'Just send me some literature first').

If you talk about the meeting in terms of *working with* the customer (not doing something to them), this will ring more bells with them: 'It's an opportunity for you to work out together how best ... '

Overall, you are seeking to create a feeling of customer orientation, describing something useful to them and doing so in a personalised way (not sounding like the 'standard spiel'). If the feeling is right, you can move on:

4 Request a specific time

You need to ask directly for an appointment. Indeed, there is simply no time to beat about the bush doing anything else.

> *You will be most successful if you:*
>
> • mention the duration of the meeting
> • respect their time and schedule
> • offer alternative times

So:

• *mention the duration of the meeting.* Honestly. It is no good pretending that 30 minutes is sufficient time if manifestly it transpires that an hour is necessary. At worst, the customer will allow the exact time stated and then say they must go because they have another appointment – and the sales person will not thank you for that;

• *give the customer adequate lead time.* They are less likely to refuse an appointment 7–10 days hence than one for tomorrow. Remember that it is their timescale that matters, not yours. Of course, an immediate appointment is nice, but bear in mind that your urgent need to sell is probably greater than their need to buy;

• *offer alternative times.* This reduces the likelihood of a 'no', prompting them to choose one or another. 'Would 3.30 on the afternoon of Thursday 22nd suit, or would Friday 23rd be better?' This has the first option stated more precisely than the second; and you can always go on to two more (and then two more again), varying the degrees of precision: 'In that case, would Monday the following week be suitable, or would it be better later in that week?'

Think about productivity as you suggest times: for example, a meeting at 9 a.m. (or even occasionally at 8.30) rather than 9.30 a.m., may help squeeze one more appointment into a particular day (and the customer may prefer such times at which they are not interrupting something). However, it must always sound as if customers' convenience is more important to you than yours. A hackneyed approach along the lines of: 'John will be in your area on Thursday' will be unlikely to be believed, and could do more harm than good as it seems you are ranking your convenience above theirs.

5 Deal with objections
Sometimes, of course, resistance will be met. Your job then is to deal with or bypass the objection, getting back on track so that an appointment can still be made.

One example that demonstrates the possibilities is called the boomerang technique, which turns an objection to your advantage:

Prospect: 'It really isn't convenient. I just don't have time.'

You: 'It's because I understand you're busy that I think a short meeting would be helpful ... ', returning to a description of how a meeting would help them, and perhaps contrasting that positively with other ways of going about finding out.

There are more examples of objection-handling methods in the Thursday section which will not be repeated here.

6 Thanks and confirmation
1 *Externally.* With objections past and a time agreed, you should summarise briefly what will now happen. 'Right, I will

put that brochure in the post to you, Mr Brown, and make sure John is at your offices at 2.30 p.m. on Wednesday week – that's the 15th.' Nothing more may be required. However, it is sometimes appropriate, and appreciated, to promise, and then organise, written confirmation.

Courtesy costs nothing, and attention to confirmation factors marks you as efficient as well as polite.

2 *Internally.* You must remember to action anything agreed ahead of the meeting, and make – and pass on if necessary – suitable notes about the customer, the conversation and the timing agreed. Sometimes, additional administrative details may be valuable; indeed, these may directly assist the sales person making the visit. Just one small point, for example, asking about, noting and passing on information about where to park, can save significant time and frustration.

But we have neglected one stage, that involving the questions you doubtless need to ask. This is because its place in the sequence of events described is less certain. It may go between stages 3 and 4 or be just ahead of the agreement phase occurring between stages 5 and 6; or questions may need to be spread throughout the process. Wherever it fits in, it is important.

Asking questions

Often, questions are a prerequisite to fixing and having a good meeting. The answers produce information that assist in planning the meeting that will take place. Equally important, being asked questions may persuade the prospect that they are being treated like an individual and that the subsequent meeting will also be tailored to their needs.

A checklist may help you here, and can act as a prompt preventing key things being overlooked in the heat of the moment.

Time is not on your side here. Questions must be well phrased and get straight to the point, and everything that is said must be tailored to the customer's viewpoint. Customers, if they are interested at all, want you to know and understand sufficiently so that the meeting that follows is well matched to their needs. But they do not want a lengthy, vague set of questions; they do not want the Spanish Inquisition.

Good, businesslike questioning actually allows you to create a positive impression of someone in an organisation who knows their job.

Accurate liaison

Always – but always – pass on information accurately. Whoever is at the subsequent meeting is going to look silly if they ask something only to be told: 'I spent five minutes going through that with your colleague.' Making it look as if the right hand does not know what the left hand is doing is no way to sell anything.

Summary

So, telephoning to try to set up appointments is not the easiest of calls to make. You do not want to come over as 'pushy', yet you need to set out to achieve what you want. The best way to do this is to follow the stages summarised as follows:

The stages of the appointment-making call

1 A greeting.
2 Identification.
3 Quoting reasons for calling.
4 Requesting a specific timed appointment.
5 Dealing with objections.
6 Thanks and confirmation.
7 Questions – as required.

Such an approach will certainly make the process easier and the result more certain. It will also help make your call the kind which is acceptable and more likely to be listened to – and acted on.

Well executed, such calls are very powerful in their impact. They not only arrange meetings, which is their immediate purpose, but they also set up those meetings – actually starting the process of making the meetings in question successful.

The customer's view
Imagine the customer just prior to the meeting. They may well be expecting someone they have never met. The appointment may now be on a day that is busier than they expected (a situation that might be labelled 'normal'). So they are likely saying to themselves 'What will this be like? Will it be a waste of time or will it be useful?' How can they tell? Well, probably they cannot. But it will help put them in the right frame of mind if they are able to recall an efficient and, to their mind, appropriate first contact: 'The person who rang me seemed to know what they were talking about. They asked sensible questions, and seemed most concerned to be sure I would find the meeting useful ... should be all right. Anyway, let's see what they have to say.'

Such reflections can do no harm and may actively assist; more so if, in a real conversation, there are more specific things to recall that ring bells with them.

The week in summary

During the week, we have covered a variety of aspects of telephone selling, and reviewed three different types of call. Here is a summary of the key common elements that act to make any call effective.

Before the call

Be prepared: the foundation of success

- Set clear objectives
- Know your product/service
- Think through descriptions
- Anticipate objections
- Remember the short duration of calls
- Aim to compensate for the voice-only factor

During the call

Use your voice: your greatest asset

- To create a rapport
- To sound efficient
- To create emphasis
- To inject enthusiasm

Direct the call: keeping control

- Keep your objective in mind
- Use an organised approach
- Prevent sidetracking
- Keep the customer in mind

Be persuasive: to achieve your objective

- Establish the need
- Paint a picture
- Talk benefits
- Match the case to the individual customer
- Rebalance to overcome objections
- Take the initiative in closing

After the call

> *Be efficient: to secure all you have done*
>
> • Record and confirm everything necessary
>
> *Recognise the dynamic nature of the process*
>
> • Be conscious of what you do and how it works
> • Be prepared to learn from experience, and adapt what you do to future customer demands, expectations and situations

Sales success is rarely, if ever, a simple matter. Still less is it achieved through a magic formula (if only!). You may never win them all, but success comes about through attention to detail, through maximising the effectiveness of every stage of the process, so that cumulatively the customer is led irresistibly towards saying 'Yes'.

A considered, customer-orientated and systematic approach is most likely to be successful.

NOTES

NOTES

Further *Successful Business in a Week* **titles from Hodder & Stoughton and the Institute of Management all at £6.99**

All Hodder & Stoughton books are available from your local bookshop or can be ordered direct from the publisher. Just tick the titles you want and fill in the form below. Prices and availability subject to change without notice.

To: Hodder & Stoughton Ltd, Cash Sales Department, Bookpoint, 39 Milton Park, Abingdon, Oxon, OX14 4TD. If you have a credit card you may order by telephone – 01235 400414.

E-mail address: orders@bookpoint.co.uk

Please enclose a cheque or postal order made payable to Bookpoint Ltd to the value of the cover price and allow the following for postage and packaging:

UK & BFPO: £4.30 for one book; £6.30 for two books; £8.30 for three books.

OVERSEAS & EIRE: £4.80 for one book; £7.10 for 2 or 3 books (surface mail).

Name: ....

Address: ....

....

If you would prefer to pay by credit card, please complete:

Please debit my Visa/Mastercard/Diner's Card/American Express (delete as appropriate) card no:

❏❏❏❏❏❏❏❏❏❏❏❏❏❏❏❏❏❏

Signature .... Expiry Date ....